Organizing and Collecting

The Number System

Nina Liu
Maarten Dolk
Catherine Twomey Fosnot

DEDICATED TO TEACHERS™

*first*hand
An imprint of Heinemann
361 Hanover Street
Portsmouth, NH 03801–3912
firsthand.heinemann.com

Offices and agents throughout the world

ISBN 13: 978-0-325-01011-3
ISBN 10: 0-325-01011-0

SCHOOL PUBLISHERS

Harcourt School Publishers
6277 Sea Harbor Drive
Orlando, FL 32887–6777
www.harcourtschool.com

ISBN 13: 978-0-15-360563-5
ISBN 10: 0-15-360563-4

© 2007 Catherine Twomey Fosnot

The development of a portion of the material described within was supported in part by the National Science Foundation under Grant No. 9911841. Any opinions, findings, and conclusions or recommendations expressed in these materials are those of the authors and do not necessarily reflect the views of the National Science Foundation.

Library of Congress Cataloging-in-Publication Data
CIP data is on file with the Library of Congress

Printed in the United States of America on acid-free paper

14 15 16 17   ML   12 13 14 15

Acknowledgements

Photography

Herbert Seignoret
Mathematics in the City, City College of New York

Illustrator

Terri Murphy

Schools featured in photographs

The Muscota New School/PS 314 (an empowerment school in Region 10), New York, NY
Independence School/PS 234 (Region 9), New York, NY
Fort River Elementary School, Amherst, MA

Contents

Unit Overview

This unit begins with the story of the Masloppy family—an endearing, large family that finds it difficult to keep track of things. Everyone is forever losing, misplacing, and looking for things. One of the children, Nicholas, decides to sort, organize, and take inventory of things in the house. He counts and bundles materials and labels containers and baskets, and life in the Masloppy household is smoother thereafter.

The idea of taking inventory is brought to the classroom, where children work to count and label baskets of supplies and materials. The discussion focuses on organizing in groups and skip-counting, then specifically on groups of ten. The concept of place value is developed as the children pack objects into groups of ten and study patterns in the data. There are opportunities to deepen their understanding by packing in fives and playing games that focus on groups of ten, and there are minilessons that use the ten-frame as a visual model of five and ten. (The structure of the ten-frame is similar to that of the arithmetic rack, which is discussed

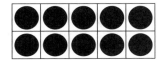

ten-frame

The Landscape of Learning

BIG IDEAS

- Compensation and equivalence
- Place determines values
- Place value patterns occur when making and adding on groups of ten
- Unitizing
- Commutativity and associativity

STRATEGIES

- Using synchrony and one-to-one tagging
- Skip-counting
- Keeping one addend whole, using landmark numbers, and/or taking leaps of ten
- Counting on and counting backward
- Using the five- and ten-structures
- Making ten
- Splitting

MODEL

- Ten-frame

in *The Double-Decker Bus,* another unit in the *Contexts for Learning Mathematics* series. Both use five and ten as landmark numbers: the arithmetic rack has four groups of five arranged in two rows of ten, the ten frame has two groups of five. The ten-frame is used in this unit because it more closely resembles the context of packing.) In the second week the inventory context is extended to include ordering more classroom supplies as a way to develop and support addition strategies, which include jumping to friendly numbers (multiples of ten) and jumping by ten.

As children pack and count groups of items, they begin to unitize—to count groups and objects at the same time. Children develop an understanding of place value as they construct the idea that the number of packs and loose items is related to the total number of objects and that the numbers change when items are added to make full packs or when a pack of ten is added.

The game Collecting Stamps and its variations are included in this unit. These can be played throughout the year as a way for children to develop place value and addition strategies. The game and its variations extend composing and decomposing strategies while promoting understanding of equivalence—for example, representing 26 + 8 as equal to 26 + 4 + 4.

The Mathematical Landscape

This unit was designed to support the development of an understanding of the Hindu-Arabic number system, including counting, unitizing, and place value. The model introduced in this unit is the ten-frame. It enables children to move away from counting one by one, toward decomposing and composing number with subunits. It encourages the automatizing of basic facts and develops addition strategies by focusing on relationships. These include strategies such as making ten (19 + 7 = 20 + 6) and jumping by ten (27 + 11 = 27 + 10 + 1).

This unit is designed to encourage the development of some of the big ideas underlying early number sense:

❖ *compensation and equivalence*

❖ *unitizing*

❖ *place determines value*

❖ *commutativity and associativity*

❖ *place value patterns occur when making and adding on groups of ten*

❖ Compensation and equivalence

Children may initially have a difficult time comprehending that 5 + 3 is equivalent to 4 + 4. The big ideas here are compensation and equivalence—that if you lose one (from the five, for example) but gain it elsewhere (onto the three), the total stays the same. These big ideas, once constructed, allow children to realize that a problem like 19 + 21 can be solved with a double, 20 + 20.

❖ Unitizing

Unitizing requires that children use number to count not only objects but also groups—and to count them both simultaneously. For young learners, unitizing is a shift in perspective. Children have just learned to count ten objects, one by one. Unitizing these ten things as *one* thing—one group—challenges their original idea of number. How can something be ten and one at the same time?

As children develop the ability to see five as a subunit you may begin to see them count the number of groups of five. For example, they may say fifteen is three groups of five. Here they are unitizing; they are treating the five as a group, counted as one—one group of five.

❖ Place determines value

The idea that a digit can represent (for example) ones or tens or hundreds depending on where it is placed, is what we mean by place value. The digit 2 represents two units, but the units themselves can change; they can be ones or tens or hundreds or more. The unit varies. The value it represents changes depending on the column in which it is placed.

❖ Commutativity and associativity

Algebraically, commutativity for addition is represented as $a + b = b + a$, and associativity for addition is represented as $(a + b) + c = a + (b + c)$. Children need many opportunities to compose and decompose numbers before they come to realize that numbers can be grouped in a variety of ways, or presented in a different order, and the amounts stay the same. Although children may have constructed these ideas with small numbers by the time they start working with this unit, they often need to revisit these ideas when they begin to explore place value. The equivalence of 2 sets of 10 items and 3 loose items, to 1 ten and 13 loose, can at first be somewhat elusive.

❖ Place value patterns occur when making and adding on groups of ten

Once children have an understanding of the landmark decade numbers in our number system, they can easily count forward by 10: 10, 20, 30, etc. But adding 10 onto a number when the unit amount is not zero (e.g., 32) is not as easy. Children are frequently surprised by the pattern that results when adding 10—42, 52, 62, 72, etc. This pattern and the reason for its occurrence constitute an important big idea connected to place value; this idea is critical to the development of efficient addition strategies. For example, in solving 42 + 19, we often want children to just think: 52, 62, minus 1, 61. But without a deep knowledge of place value and the patterns that result when adding ten, children cannot easily apply this strategy.

As you work with the activities in this unit, you will notice that children use many strategies to organize and count objects. Here are some strategies to notice:

❖ *using synchrony and one-to-one tagging*

❖ *counting on and counting backward*

❖ *skip-counting*

❖ *using the five- and ten-structures*

❖ *making ten*

❖ *keeping one addend whole, using landmark numbers, and/or taking leaps of ten*

❖ *splitting*

❖ Using synchrony and one-to-one tagging

Counting effectively requires children to coordinate many actions simultaneously. Not only must they remember the word that comes next, they must use only one word for each object (synchrony) and tag each object once and only once (one-to-one tagging). When children are learning to count, this coordination is initially very difficult; they often skip some objects, double-tag others, and are not synchronized, using too many or too few words for the number of objects they are counting.

❖ Counting on and counting backward

A major landmark strategy to notice and celebrate is when a child begins to count on—for example, to solve 8 + 9, the child labels the first set 8, moves it to the side as a group, and then continues with 9, 10, and on to 17. It is the developing understanding of the relationship of the parts and the whole that causes this shift in strategy. For subtraction, children also become able to count backward until they reach the target amount, knowing that these amounts together make the whole. For example, solving 17 − 8 by counting backward: 17, 16, 15, 14, 13, 12, 11, 10. Children remove the 8 (either mentally or by physically removing 8 objects) and realize that there are 9 left and that 9 + 8 = 17.

❖ Skip-counting

As children move to the strategy of making groups when they count, they need to know that each group must contain the same number of objects and that the number by which they count has to be exactly the same as the number of objects in each group. When children are new to skip-counting, they sometimes use a rote sequence they know regardless of the number of items in a group. For example, when the groups contain only five objects, they might skip-count by ten. Or when the groups contain 10 objects but there are 8 left over, children may continue to count the 8 as a group of ten. They may also have difficulty skip-counting beyond 100.

❖ Using the five- and ten-structures

One of the most important ways of structuring number is to compose and decompose numbers into groups of five and ten. For example, seeing 8 as 5 + 3, or 7 as 5 + 2, is very helpful in automatizing the basic fact "8 + 7." Since 3 + 2 also equals 5, 8 + 7 is equivalent to 3 fives. The five-structure is also helpful in automatizing all the combinations that make ten— if 6 is equivalent to 5 + 1, then only 4 more are needed to make 2 fives, which equal 10.

❖ Making ten

Using the combinations of whole numbers that add up to ten is a powerful strategy that makes learning most of the more difficult basic facts easier. If children know that 8 + 2 is equivalent to 10, then it is quite easy to solve for 8 + 7. They simply take 2 from the 7 and give it to the 8. This produces 10 + 5.

❖ Keeping one addend whole, using landmark numbers, and/or taking leaps of ten

As children develop an understanding of place value, you will want to encourage them to make use of the place value patterns for computation. One of the first strategies to encourage is using landmark numbers and taking leaps of ten. For example, 33 + 29 can be solved as 43, 53, plus 7 to get to 60 (a landmark), plus 2 more. Taking leaps of ten develops into taking leaps of multiples of ten, e.g., the ability to add 29 by adding 30 − 1. The problem can also be solved by turning it into 32 + 30 or by first adding 7 to 33 to get to the landmark number of 40, thus producing the easier problem of 40 + 22. Having a deep understanding of landmark numbers and operations is the hallmark of computing with numeracy.

❖ Splitting

Another important strategy to encourage is splitting—decomposing by splitting the columns and making use of partial sums. For example, 33 + 29 can be solved as 30 + 20 + 3 + 9. This strategy is not only important for mental arithmetic; it is a precursor to the development of the regrouping algorithms (Kamii 1985).

It is important for you to notice these emerging strategies and celebrate children's developing number sense. A long-term objective on the horizon of the landscape of learning for addition is for children to look to the numbers first before deciding on a strategy. Mathematicians do not use the same strategy for every problem; their approaches vary depending on the numbers. Note when children begin to diversify their strategies and search for efficiency. The justification for doing so is rooted in the big ideas of the commutative and associative properties and on a good sense of landmark numbers.

MATHEMATICAL MODELING

The model used in this unit is the ten-frame. Models go through three stages of development (Gravemeijer 1999; Fosnot and Dolk 2001):

❖ *model of the situation*

❖ *model of children's strategies*

❖ *model as a tool for thinking*

❖ Model of the situation

The ten-frame with ten dots is introduced in this unit as a model of a group of ten objects. The ten-frame also incorporates the five-structure to enable children to explore the relationship between the five- and ten-structures. The ten-frame is introduced in the context of making packs of ten as children take inventory of their classroom supplies.

❖ Model of children's strategies

Children benefit from seeing the teacher model their strategies. Once a model has been introduced to represent a situation, you can use it to display the children's strategies as they determine arrangements of dots on the ten-frame. Use a marker to draw on an overhead projection of the ten-frame the groups that the children saw and used to compute.

❖ Model as a tool for thinking

Eventually children will be able to use the model as a tool for thinking—they will be able to see 7 as 5 + 2, with 3 more needed to make 10. Over time, the ten-frame can become an important model to support children in learning the basic combinations of numbers that sum to ten.

Many opportunities to discuss these landmarks in mathematical development will arise as you work through the unit. Look for moments of puzzlement. Don't hesitate to let children discuss their ideas and check and recheck their counting. Celebrate their accomplishments! These are developmental milestones.

A graphic of the full landscape of learning for early number sense, addition, and subtraction is provided on page 10. The purpose of the graphic is to enable you to see the longer journey of children's mathematical development and to place your work with this unit within the scope of this long-term development. You may also find it helpful to use this graphic as a way to record the progress of individual children for yourself. Each landmark can be shaded in as you find evidence in a child's work and in what the child says—evidence that a landmark strategy, big idea, or way of modeling has been constructed. In a sense you will be recording the individual pathways children take as they develop as young mathematicians.

References and Resources

Dolk, Maarten, and Catherine Twomey Fosnot. 2004a. *Addition and Subtraction Minilessons, Grades PreK–3.* CD-ROM with accompanying facilitator's guide by Antonia Cameron, Sherrin B. Hersch, and Catherine Twomey Fosnot. Portsmouth, NH: Heinemann.

———. 2004b. *Fostering Children's Mathematical Development, Grades PreK–3: The Landscape of Learning.* CD-ROM with accompanying facilitator's guide by Sherrin B. Hersch, Antonia Cameron, and Catherine Twomey Fosnot. Portsmouth, NH: Heinemann.

———. 2004c. *Taking Inventory, Grades PreK–3: The Role of Context.* CD-ROM with accompanying facilitator's guide by Antonia Cameron, Sherrin B. Hersch, and Catherine Twomey Fosnot. Portsmouth, NH: Heinemann.

Fosnot, Catherine Twomey, and Maarten Dolk. 2001. *Young Mathematicians at Work: Constructing Number Sense, Addition, and Subtraction.* Portsmouth, NH: Heinemann.

Gravemeijer, Koeno P.E. 1999. How emergent models may foster the constitution of formal mathematics. *Mathematical Thinking and Learning* 1(2), 155–77.

Kamii, Constance. 1985. *Young Children Reinvent Arithmetic.* New York, NY: Teachers College Press.

Weyl, H. Quoted in "Mathematics and the Laws of Nature." In *The Armchair Science Reader,* S. Sorkin and I. S. Gordon. 1959. New York: Simon and Schuster.

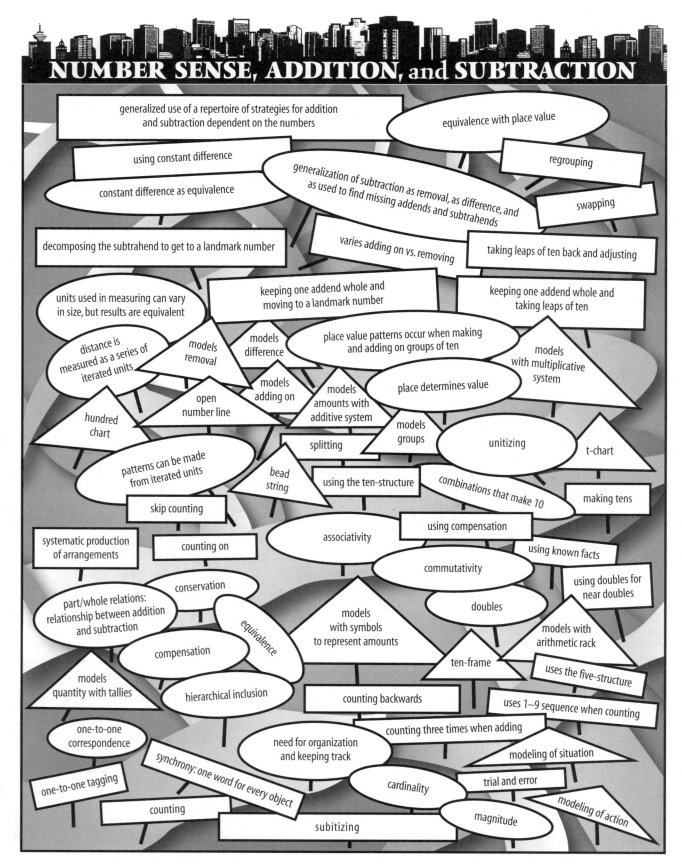

NUMBER SENSE, ADDITION, and SUBTRACTION

generalized use of a repertoire of strategies for addition and subtraction dependent on the numbers

equivalence with place value

using constant difference

regrouping

constant difference as equivalence

generalization of subtraction as removal, as difference, and as used to find missing addends and subtrahends

swapping

decomposing the subtrahend to get to a landmark number

varies adding on vs. removing

taking leaps of ten back and adjusting

units used in measuring can vary in size, but results are equivalent

keeping one addend whole and moving to a landmark number

keeping one addend whole and taking leaps of ten

distance is measured as a series of iterated units

models removal

models difference

place value patterns occur when making and adding on groups of ten

models with multiplicative system

hundred chart

open number line

models adding on

models amounts with additive system

place determines value

models groups

unitizing

t-chart

patterns can be made from iterated units

bead string

splitting

using the ten-structure

combinations that make 10

making tens

skip counting

systematic production of arrangements

counting on

associativity

using compensation

using known facts

commutativity

using doubles for near doubles

part/whole relations: relationship between addition and subtraction

conservation

equivalence

compensation

models with symbols to represent amounts

doubles

models with arithmetic rack

models quantity with tallies

hierarchical inclusion

ten-frame

uses the five-structure

counting backwards

uses 1–9 sequence when counting

one-to-one correspondence

counting three times when adding

need for organization and keeping track

modeling of situation

one-to-one tagging

synchrony: one word for every object

cardinality

trial and error

modeling of action

counting

subitizing

magnitude

The landscape of learning: number sense, addition, and subtraction on the horizon showing landmark strategies (rectangles), big ideas (ovals), and models (triangles).

Taking Inventory

The context of organizing and taking inventory of classroom materials is developed with the story *The Masloppy Family*. After you read the story, the class discusses how Nicholas organized his family's things and how his strategies might be helpful for keeping track of things in the classroom. Children then team up to determine the quantities of various items found in the classroom.

Day One Outline

Developing the Context

☀ Read *The Masloppy Family* and explain to the children that they will work with partners to take inventory of some of the materials in the classroom.

Supporting the Investigation

☀ Note children's strategies and help them consider ways to organize the objects and keep track of their counts.

Preparing for the Math Congress

☀ Plan to focus the congress on strategies that will help children work more efficiently when they continue taking inventory on Day Two.

Facilitating the Math Congress

☀ Generate discussion on a few children's strategies and record them on chart paper.

Materials Needed

The Masloppy Family
[If you do not have the full-color read-aloud book (available from Heinemann), you can use Appendix A.]

Baskets of sorted objects (e.g., books, manipulatives, writing tools, art and office supplies) organized in the quantities suggested on page 13.

Large rubber bands, paper clips, and/or small bags to bundle materials, as needed

Drawing paper—several sheets per pair of children

Clipboards—one per pair of children

Large chart pad and easel (or chalkboard or whiteboard)

Markers

Developing the Context

☀ Read *The Masloppy Family* and explain to the children that they will work with partners to take inventory of some of the materials in the classroom.

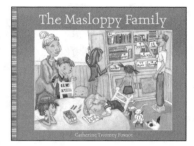

Start by reading *The Masloppy Family* (Appendix A). Have the children discuss how Nicholas helped his family organize things in his house. If no one brings it up, remind the class how Nicholas used a rubber band to bundle ten pencils together, and how he labeled and recorded the count for various items. You can also mention that people who work in stores do the same thing from time to time so they know exactly what they have in stock and what they might need to order. Tell the children this is called "taking inventory."

Ask the children to consider how Nicholas' strategies might help the class take inventory of its own materials. Knowing how many items in each category are kept in the classroom is important as a way to keep track of materials and to know when materials are lost or when more need to be ordered. Show the class several baskets of materials that you have already sorted, such as books and markers, and ask, "What other materials in our classroom could we inventory?" List the children's ideas, such as pens, pencils, crayons, scissors, stickers, books, puzzles, blocks, connecting cubes, folders, and bags.

Tell the class that you've already sorted some of these materials into baskets and today they can begin there. Assign pairs of children to work with different materials at different stations around the classroom. Set up the work stations around the room so children will have sufficient space to work. Offer each pair of children paper and a clipboard to help them track and record, but don't specify how the paper is to be used. As children count, they will need to make decisions about what and how to record.

Differentiating Instruction

Use what you already know about individual children to match them with appropriate materials and quantities. Think about possibilities for challenges. Materials like blocks or math manipulatives present a natural need for organization. Connecting cubes can be put in towers of five or ten and may encourage children who lose track to grapple with ways to organize. Some may try skip-counting by twos. Other materials such as paper bags, construction paper, markers, or pencils might be bundled with rubber bands or paper clips into larger groups of ten, providing children with opportunities to develop unitizing (counting groups as units) and place value. It is tempting to give children who are still struggling with the counting sequence only small numbers of objects in order to simplify their task, but although this choice may increase their chances of success in getting correct answers, it will not allow them to examine the sequence and patterns in our number system. For example, to develop an understanding that the digits go 1 to 9 between the decades, that the decades themselves have a pattern (30, 40, 50, etc.), and that some numbers are landmarks (e.g., 50 and 100), children need the experience of working with fairly large amounts and making many repeated attempts to count and recount them.

It is also important to make this activity as genuine as possible. Don't just put small amounts in baskets and have children count and label. They will see right through such an ordinary counting activity. The purpose of taking inventory is to provide a realistic experience in which keeping track, determining quantity, and recording are important—not because the teacher asked for this information, but because it is important to know.

Here are suggested ranges of numbers for organizing materials:

- Baskets of books—between 10 and 50 per basket, perhaps sorted by genre or topic
- Baskets or bags of math manipulatives such as connecting cubes, pattern blocks, puzzle pieces—between 40 and 120 per basket or bag
- Baskets of writing tools (pencils, markers, crayons) and art supplies—between 30 and 250 per basket

As you pair children, consider that slight differences in ability can help both children grow, while big differences in ability can limit potential for growth. Consider:

- Will this child need support with counting by ones, or does he or she skip-count fluently?
- Will this child's learning be solidified by explaining or clarifying his or her thinking?
- Is the range in ability of two children too great to be constructive?

Supporting the Investigation

As children work, circulate around the room. Listen to children as they make decisions and note how they are organizing, keeping track, and determining quantities. Pay attention to what and how they are recording.

✦ How do they organize for counting? Do they move or line up objects as a way to keep track of objects they have counted or do they count the same objects over again? As you confer, you might ask them to consider how they will know which ones they have counted and which they haven't.

✦ Do they make groups of equal sizes (such as groups of five or ten) as a helpful way to determine quantity, or do they group only by color or other attributes? This latter strategy shows some desire to sort and organize what is being counted but not necessarily a consciousness of grouping strategies related to the number system. As numbers become greater, children may lose track of their count if they are counting by ones. As you confer, you might ask if there is a way to organize the materials that might help them track their count more easily.

☀ Note children's strategies and help them consider ways to organize the objects and keep track of their counts.

- ✦ Does their organizing strategy help to count the objects? Children may organize their materials one way but use a different strategy to count—e.g., make groups of five but count by ones. Support them by asking how many are in one group, then two, then three; ask them to predict how many there might be if another group was made; then let them check their guess.

- ✦ How do they count? If they are skip-counting, is it rote or are the numbers increasing by exactly the same number as the size of the group? For example, do they say 10 even when there are only 3 items left? What happens when they go beyond 100? Do they revert to ones or continue to skip-count by tens?

- ✦ Do they add groups and use subtotals? For example, "10 and 10—that's 20, then 10 more is 30, and then 2 more is 32."

- ✦ Are any children unitizing? Are they counting the number of groups as well as the number in the group? Notice if they correlate the number of tens with the number of objects. For example, if they are unitizing they might say, "5 tens—that's 50." As children discuss numbers, check for understanding about number: "When you say 20, do you mean 20 cubes or 20 tens?"

Children's recordings often give clues about their number sense. As children work, note how they record their work. Do they track their count, writing down subtotals, for instance? Do they use tallies or symbols, or do they use numerals? How do they write numbers? A child who records 27 objects as "207" is likely in the very early stages of developing place value. Rather than seeing only the fact that this is incorrect, note that it actually represents an understanding of 27 as 20 plus 7.

Sample Children's Work

Often children are not willing to let the numerals stand for the quantity alone. They need to draw the objects as well. Reversals are also common at this point in development. *[See Figure 1]* Amanda's representation of the quantity is evidence that she thinks of 120 as 100 plus 20. *[See Figure 2]* She understands the quantity but has not yet constructed place value.

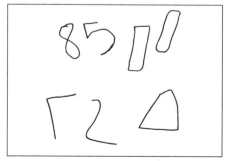

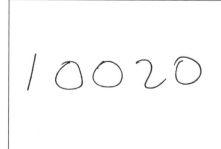

Figure 1 *85 long and 27 triangular blocks.*   Figure 2 *120 cubes.*

Conferring with Children at Work

Seth and Susanne are taking inventory of the connecting cubes. They have sorted and linked together the cubes by color. Seth is counting on the top row.

Seth: … 28, 29, 30, 31, 32, 33, 34, 35, 36, 37, 38, 39… um, 50.

Susanne: No, it's 39, 40.

Seth: OK—39, 40, 41, 42, 43, 44, 45, 46, 47, 48, 49… what's after 49?

Susanne: *(Looks up in the air and recites.)* It goes 20, 30, 40, 50. So it's 49, 50.

Seth: 50, 51, 52. Whew. There's 52 cubes.

Nina (the teacher): Susanne, I noticed you used skip-counting by ten to help you figure what comes after 49. How did that help?

Susanne: Well, every time you say something-nine, it can't be something-ten next. So the next one is like 10, 20, 30, 40, 50.

Nina: That's an important thing to notice. After 9, it's a new something? And then it goes 1 to 9 again? I wonder…is there a way you can organize the cubes and mark the one-to-nines and the "somethings" so that it's easier to keep track and to count? Maybe we could bundle these amounts in towers and attach a sticky note to the tower that says what the "something" is.

Susanne: You mean we could make towers of ten?

Nina: Yes, you could attach a sticky note to the first tower of ten and write 10. What would the next tower be?

Author's Notes

Seth and Susanne have sorted the cubes by color, not amounts. They have not thought to use grouping as they count.

Seth counts easily to 39 and from 41 to 59, but he struggles when crossing the decades, from 39 to 40 and again from 49 to 50. This is a different kind of struggle than the struggle of a child who doesn't know what comes after 14 or 26, who is still constructing the pattern of one to nine in the counting sequence. In both cases, children need more experience with counting larger numbers.

Nina notes that Susanne has linked the crossing of the decades to skip-counting by ten. By asking Susanne to explain her thinking, Nina hopes to help Seth think more clearly about counting across decades. Nina also helps Susanne think about organizing in groups of ten, rather than by color, in order to count by ten.

Preparing for the Math Congress

As the end of the workshop period nears, remind children to write on their papers their names, and the basket they worked on. They will be using these papers again, so it might be a good idea to leave the clipboards by the baskets they were working on. Ask the children to think about the strategies they found helpful for keeping track and for determining how many objects there were. Explain that in a few minutes you want them all to come to the meeting area for a brief discussion of some of the strategies they found helpful.

☀ Plan to focus the congress on strategies that will help children work more efficiently when they continue taking inventory on Day Two.

Tips for Structuring the Math Congress

Consider asking several pairs of children to describe what they did. You may want to choose children who overcame a hurdle—for example, losing track when counting by ones, or struggling with skip-counting. Some children may have decided to make groups of five, two, or ten. Look for interesting strategies or struggles to discuss that will help other children as they continue to take inventory on Day Two.

Facilitating the Math Congress

☀ Generate discussion on a few children's strategies and record them on chart paper.

This will be a brief discussion, not a full math congress. The point is only to generate discussion of a few of the strategies that children tried. As children share, write their ideas down on chart paper. On Day Two you can start with a reminder of several of the ideas charted.

Assessment Tips

As you moved around the room today supporting children as they determined quantities of various objects, you had many opportunities to observe their counting and grouping strategies as well as the ways they were notating amounts—i.e., the strategies they were using at the beginning of this unit. Make notes about your observations, date them, and place the notes in the children's portfolios.

Reflections on the Day

Today, children heard a story about organizing materials and ways to keep track of them. Then they started to take inventory of supplies in their own classroom. This context provided ample opportunities for children to count large numbers of items, keeping track of the count, and organizing both the counting and the recording. On Day Two they will continue sharing a few of the strategies they found helpful and then take inventory of other materials in the classroom.

Continuing the Inventory

The day begins with a brief reminder of some of the ways children tried to organize items on Day One. After reviewing the strategies used on Day One, children continue with their inventory of classroom supplies.

Day Two Outline

Supporting the Investigation

※ Remind children of the inventory task and introduce paper clips, rubber bands, and small bags as optional tools for today's investigation.

※ As children continue taking inventory, note whether they are using more efficient strategies than on Day One.

Preparing for the Math Congress

※ Plan to focus the congress on some of the ways children have grouped and counted.

Facilitating the Math Congress

※ Invite one or two pairs of children to demonstrate and explain their counting strategies. Check for understanding by having one or two other children paraphrase the strategy that was shared.

Materials Needed

Chart of strategies from Day One

Baskets of sorted objects from Day One

Large rubber bands, paper clips, and/or small bags to bundle materials

Clipboards with children's work from Day One

Drawing paper—several sheets per pair of children

Boxes of bandages, plastic bags, or garbage bags that display totals on the package

Markers

Supporting the Investigation

☀ Remind children of the inventory task and introduce paper clips, rubber bands, and small bags as optional tools for today's investigation.

☀ As children continue taking inventory, note whether they are using more efficient strategies than on Day One.

Start by gathering children in the meeting area. Remind them of the inventory task that they started on Day One and the ideas they shared in the brief discussion afterward. Since it is likely that several children began to group items as a way to keep track on Day One, introduce paper clips, rubber bands, and small bags as optional tools for the day's work, as a way of encouraging more children to group items today. Have children then return to their inventory task from Day One or start to inventory a new basket of items.

Circulate around the room as the investigation progresses, conferring with pairs of children and taking note of their organizing and counting strategies. Here are some additional things you might look for today:

Are children using different strategies than they did on Day One? Are they trying new ways to count or double-check? You might ask why they changed their methods and have them compare the two methods. What was helpful about this count? What was challenging about this count?

✦ If children are making groups, how are they counting them? Do they add the groups ("5 and 5 make 10, and 5 more make 15") or do they skip-count ("5, 10, 15, 20") or do they use a combination of both ("5, 10, 15, and here's another 5…15 plus 5 is, um, 20").

✦ Do they get different totals when they count in different ways; if so, do they recognize that one of them must be wrong? If they aren't bothered by the different counts, ask whether it's possible that there are, for instance, both 21 and 25 items in a basket. Encourage the children to recheck carefully. If they don't identify the error, ask a question that will guide their thinking. "So far you have 20. Now you have 3 more. What's 3 more than 20?" Or "Do you want to make a sign when you get to certain numbers so that you don't have to start all over again when you lose track?"

Behind the Numbers

When children start moving from counting by ones to more abstract strategies, they are prone to making errors in their count. Children who make no mistakes when counting one by one might make mistakes when counting groups or skip-counting. If children make mistakes, ask them to explain their thinking, and make sure they correct themselves as they explain. Putting too much emphasis on the correct answer, however, may cause children to cling to secure, familiar strategies and thus may actually hinder their development.

Differentiating Instruction

Continue to choose materials for various children wisely so that the activity both challenges them and supports their growth. If some children are packing materials in groups and skip-counting with ease, you might ask them to use index cards to make signs showing the total number of items, the number of packs, and the number of loose items. If they have made groups of five, see if they can predict the number of groups of ten that could be made from them. If some children have been doing this already and have begun to notice place value patterns, you might choose new things for them to inventory, items that include information on the outside of the package indicating the total number of items contained inside. For example, boxes of bandages, plastic bags, or garbage bags frequently display totals on the outside. You might show the total and ask children to predict how many groups of ten or five they think they will find when they open the box. Allow them to check their predictions. Other children may need much more time counting by ones. For these children, do not push packing. If they insist on using paper clips or rubber bands, suggest that they make small groups such as two or five. These are easier than groups of ten for children to see as a group.

Preparing for the Math Congress

After children have had a sufficient amount of time to work, ask them to prepare for a math congress to discuss some of the ways they have grouped or organized their work. Ask them to consider what they think is important and will be helpful for others. If they tried making groups, they should be prepared to describe how they grouped and counted their materials. As you survey the pairs at work, you should think about which counting strategy you would like to discuss in the math congress, and why. For instance, if some children grouped by five but counted by ten, you might discuss the strategy of counting by fives.

☀ Plan to focus the congress on some of the ways children have grouped and counted.

▨ Tips for Structuring the Math Congress

Look for pairs of children who struggled with making groups and skip-counting, or for children who rethought what they were doing—perhaps starting with packs of five and reconfiguring them into packs of ten. Depending on what the children were working on, you could focus the congress on counting by twos or on making groups of five or ten.

Facilitating the Math Congress

Ask children to bring the materials they counted to the meeting area. You might want to start by having pairs of children team up with other pairs—facing each other—and share how they organized and counted. This preliminary sharing helps children develop the ability to articulate their own as well as others' strategies.

Invite one or two pairs of children to demonstrate and explain their counting strategies. Ask the rest of the class to listen and watch carefully. After each explanation, ask the children to signal—maybe with a thumbs-up—if they could describe the pair's approach, and have one or two children paraphrase or demonstrate the strategy. If there is a mistake in the count, refrain from pointing it out, allowing other children to identify the discrepancy instead. If only a few children give a thumbs-up signal, you might ask the pair to demonstrate their method again, perhaps more slowly, in order to encourage other children to pay careful attention so that they can reconstruct the result.

☀ Invite one or two pairs of children to demonstrate and explain their counting strategies. Check for understanding by having one or two other children paraphrase the strategy that was shared.

The math congress is more than a demonstration by children of what they did. It is a forum for scaffolding and building mathematical ideas. Since the focus of this congress is on making groups and skip-counting in general, children need not have counted the same items or used the same strategy. By carefully examining the results of one or two pairs, the children will gain a deeper understanding of skip-counting, perhaps constructing it well enough to effect change in their own methods.

Listening to and paraphrasing other people's strategies can be difficult for children, especially those who have not constructed the idea of making groups and skip-counting themselves. Some children, such as those who struggle with language, may prefer to show rather than tell. The goal is to encourage children to think deeply about the mathematics, not for each child to leave with the same level of understanding.

Inside One Classroom

A Portion of the Math Congress

Author's Notes

Nina (the teacher) invites Alejandro and Makayla to show the class what they were doing with connecting cubes. On the floor are six piles of 5 cubes. The stacks of 5 are placed in groups of 2.

Alejandro: *(Pointing to two stacks of 5 at a time.)* That's 10, 20, 30.

Makayla: *(Pointing to each stack of 5.)* That's 10, 20, 30, 40, 50, 60.

The children struggle to match the skip-counting sequence to the groups they have made.

Alejandro: That's 10, 20, 30, 40. *(At 20 and 30, he points to the same group of 10.)*

Nina: So I'm wondering whether we have 30, 60, or 40 cubes here. Makayla and Alejandro, you made these groups. How did that help you?

Nina notes that there are three different answers but doesn't correct the children. Instead, she has them share their thinking.

Alejandro: We counted by 10 and I know how to count by 10.

Nina: *(Pointing to two stacks of 5.)* You counted these two together as a ...

Nina encourages the children to recognize the ten cubes—arranged in two groups of five—as one ten, unitizing the group.

Alejandro and Makayla: Ten.

Nina: *(Pointing to the next two stacks of 5.)* And these two together as a ...

Alejandro and Makayla: Ten.

Nina: *(Pointing to the last two stacks of 5.)* And these two together as a ...

Alejandro and Makayla: Ten.

continued on next page

continued from previous page

Nina: *(Pointing to a stack of 5.)* Is this one a 10?

Makayla: Yeah.

Alejandro: No.

Nina: *(Pointing to a stack of 5.)* How many are in this stack?

Alejandro: One. No, wait, there are 5.

Nina: And 5 more is …

Makayla: Ten. Because 5 and 5 is 10.

Nina: Hmmm….I'm wondering how many of you are following what Alejandro and Makayla just said. Raise your pinky if you are confused. *(She looks around and sees many children indicating they are confused.)* A lot of us are confused. Who thinks they understand what Alejandro is saying? Kate, can you explain?

Kate: They said that...there is 5 in one stack. And they made another stack of 5. And they put them together as one group to make 10. And then they did that with all the other stacks to make ... they just made stacks of 5, and he used two stacks of 5 to make a 10.

Nina: Nod your head if you understand that. Can someone else say it in your own words? Zoë, do you understand it?

Zoë: Yeah. They put two stacks in one pile, because each stack was 5. And 5 plus 5 is 10. And you don't have to look at just one stack— you can look at two at a time.

Nina: So when you skip-count these *(pointing to two stacks of 5)*, how do you count? What do you think, Makayla—can you do it one more time?

Makayla: This is 5 and 5, which is 10. *(Pointing to the first two stacks of 5.)* And 5 and 5 again is 20. *(Pointing to the next two stacks of 5.)* Plus 5 and 5 again is 30. *(Pointing at the last pair of stacks.)*

When Alejandro and Makayla disagree, Nina refrains from saying who is right, instead going back to the groups and recounting slowly.

Alejandro struggles to track what he is counting—one group or five cubes?

Nina involves the other children, bringing more voices into the conversation. By asking children to paraphrase, she gauges understanding and gives other children another opportunity to follow the reasoning.

Again Nina checks to see if any more children understand.

Nina narrows the focus to a specific big idea: when we skip-count, how many objects are in the group we are skip-counting by?

Reflections on the Day

After revisiting different ways to organize for counting, children continued to take inventory of materials. They were introduced to tools that helped them group and track items as they counted by twos, fives, and tens. In the math congress, they looked closely at strategies like making groups, skip-counting, and perhaps unitizing.

DAY THREE

Making Packs of Ten

Materials Needed

The Masloppy Family (Appendix A)

Ten-frames (Appendix B)

Before class, prepare overhead transparencies of the ten-frames listed in the string on page 23 (or you can display enlarged photocopies of the ten-frames).

Overhead projector *(optional)*

Baskets of sorted objects from Days One and Two

Large rubber bands, paper clips, and/or small bags to bundle materials

Children's work from Days One and Two

Boxes of bandages, plastic bags, or garbage bags that display totals on the package

5" x 8" index cards (lined or un-lined)—at least four per pair of children

Large chart pad and easel

Markers

Quick images using ten-frames are introduced in a minilesson today. Children then resume the inventory investigation. They revisit their counts from Days One and Two and use index cards to make signs indicating the total number of items, the number of ten-packs, and the number of loose items. The class then prepares for a math congress to be held on Day Four.

Day Three Outline

Minilesson: Quick Images

☀ Show children a full ten-frame and discuss its structure (five boxes in each row and ten boxes altogether).

☀ Display a string of quick images using ten-frames. The images have been chosen to support children in developing more efficient counting strategies.

Developing the Context

☀ Ask children to make packs of ten as they take inventory today.

☀ Begin a chart that will be used to record the results of their work. Record a sample count on the chart and show the children the three columns (for how many in all, how many packs of ten, and how many loose).

Supporting the Investigation

☀ As children work, take note of their counting strategies.

Preparing for the Math Congress

☀ Consider which numbers you will want to examine in the math congress on Day Four.

Minilesson: Quick Images (10–15 minutes)

This minilesson introduces the ten-frame, an arrangement of ten boxes organized into two groups of five (Appendix B). Dots fill some or all of the boxes in each ten-frame. Show a full ten-frame and ask children what they notice. Be sure to elicit the idea that there are five boxes in each row, and that there are ten boxes altogether.

Using an overhead projector or enlarged ten-frames, show each image for a few seconds. Ask the children to figure out how many dots they saw and how they got that number; then ask them to tell their neighbor how many dots they saw and how they know. Show each image long enough to allow children to see groups of five and ten but not long enough for children to count each dot. This time constraint pushes children who are counting each dot to shift to strategies that are more efficient. Invite a few children to share their answers with the whole group, and then move to the next quick image.

> **String of related quick images:**
>
> 5: a ten-frame with 5 dots
>
> 10: a ten-frame with 10 dots
>
> 9: a ten-frame with 9 dots
>
> 11: a ten-frame with 10 dots and a ten-frame with 1 dot
>
> 6: a ten-frame with 6 dots (5 plus 1)

☀ Show children a full ten-frame and discuss its structure (five boxes in each row and ten boxes altogether).

☀ Display a string of quick images using ten-frames. The images have been chosen to support children in developing more efficient counting strategies.

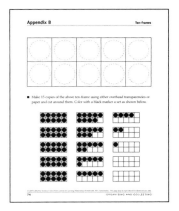

Behind the Numbers

The string starts by reinforcing the structure of the ten-frame and its subunit of five. The third image encourages the use of 10 minus 1 or 5 plus 4. The fourth image encourages counting on from 10 and the last image encourages counting on from 5.

The ten-frame resembles the structure of the red and white beads on the arithmetic rack, which is introduced in the unit *The Double-Decker Bus.* The arithmetic rack, which is used to develop number sense up to 20, can be used here as well. The arithmetic rack consists of two rows, each containing five red and five white beads. Like the ten-frame, it focuses on groups of five and ten. The only reason for using ten-frames instead of the arithmetic rack is that the ten-frames look a bit more like packs, so they fit the inventory context.

A Portion of the Minilesson

Nina (the teacher) briefly shows this quick image of nine dots.

●	●	●	●	●
●	●	●	●	

Author's Notes

This image of nine dots follows one of ten dots and one of five dots. Nina hopes that children will use those landmark numbers to figure the number in this image.

Nina: How many dots did you see? How did you know?

Ayana: I saw 9 dots.

Nina: How did you know it was 9?

Ayana: I...I don't know. I just know it's 9.

Sometimes children get an answer without knowing how they thought about it. Developing awareness of the cognitive process and sharing it makes it transparent for all children so they can consider and consciously apply these strategies when solving other problems.

Joe: I saw a line of 4 dots on the top row and another line of 4 dots on the bottom, and I know 4 plus 4 is 8. Then there was 1 more on top, so that's 9.

Nina: You used a double you knew and then added 1. Nice. Did anyone see the quick image differently?

Joe doesn't count by ones and uses a useful near-doubles strategy. However, Nina wants to ensure that landmarks are discussed so she asks for additional strategies.

Tali: I know 5 and 5 is 10, so on top there are 5 dots. Then I counted on 4 more dots—6, 7, 8, 9.

Ana: If the ten-frame was full, it would be 10. But there's 1 missing so I know it's 1 less—that's 9—and I didn't have to count every dot.

Nina: So even though the ten-frame wasn't full, you imagined that last dot there. Using the frame is helpful, isn't it? Let's see if the ten-frame can help us in this next quick image.

Nina emphasizes Ana's use of the ten-frame structure and suggests that children consider that strategy in the next image.

Developing the Context

- ☀ Ask children to make packs of ten as they take inventory today.

- ☀ Begin a chart that will be used to record the results of their work. Record a sample count on the chart and show the children the three columns (for how many in all, how many packs of ten, and how many loose).

Returning to the inventory context, remind the children how making groups can be helpful. You can also remind them how in *The Masloppy Family* Nicholas bundled together a group of ten pencils and he organized Uncle Lloyd's t-shirts in packs of five. Read the following excerpt:

> [Nicholas] *counted his pencils. Ten pencils. He put a rubber band around them and made a sign for the can they were in.*

Have a child demonstrate one such count—for example, 13 books bundled into one pack of 10 and 3 loose. Suggest that it will be helpful now if everyone makes packs of ten when they pack today. Tell them that they will record the results on a large class chart. As you prepare the chart, show the children where there are columns for how many in all, how many packs of ten, and how many loose ones. You might also want to leave space to add extra columns later on (see Days Five and Six). Ask the children to help you record the numbers for the basket of items the class just looked at together.

Item	How many in all?	How many packs of ten?	How many loose ones?
Basket A (small books)	13	1	3

Explain that when they make packs of ten today, they will record the information on index cards—the name of the item, the total number of items, how many packs of ten, and how many loose. Children should write their names on the back of the index cards. (Using blank or lined index cards allows the children to develop a notation system.) Instruct the children to use one index card per basket. When they have finished a count, they can either hold on to the index cards or attach the index cards to the baskets.

Supporting the Investigation

As children work, notice how and what they are counting. Listen carefully as they discuss the three numbers involved: the total number of items, the number of packs of ten, and the number of loose items. For children who have already organized their items in groups of ten, have them check their counts and record the counts on index cards. Have extra baskets of items available in case children finish working early, or have boxes of bags or bandages available with totals displayed on the outside to challenge them. If they know the total, can they determine the number of groups of ten?

✦ Do children count the groups of ten or do they still count by ones? If they are packing in groups of ten but still counting individual items, support them by asking, "How many are in one pack? How many are in a second pack? If there are 10 here and 10 here, how many do you think there are if we counted all the items?"

✦ Do children add the groups? For example, "5 and 5 make 10, and 5 and 5 more is 10 more. 10 and 10, that's 20." Or do they skip-count— for example, "5, 10, 15, 20"—or use a combination of skip-counting and adding?

☀ As children work, take note of their counting strategies.

- When children discuss numbers, are they talking about the number of groups or the number of items? If they do not specify, check for understanding by asking, "When you say 20, do you mean 20 cubes or 20 tens?"

- Are the children unitizing? Do they recognize that they are dealing with both one bundle of ten and ten items at the same time? Can they talk about the two numbers interchangeably? Notice if they correlate the number of tens with the number of objects—for example, they might say, "5 tens—that's 50."

- Are the children making the maximum number of groups of ten, or do they make some groups of ten but leave more than 10 loose ones?

Conferring with Children at Work

Inside One Classroom

Author's Notes

Elisa and Max are counting paper bags. They have bundled them with rubber bands into packs of 10 and are skip-counting by ten.

Max: ... 170, 180, 190, 200, 201 ...

Elisa: That's 210. So 210, 220, 230, 240. Wait. *(Pointing to 9 loose bags.)* It's 249. *(Writes 249.)*

Nina (the teacher): So you have 249 bags. How many packs do you have?

Max: We have 249.

Nina: You counted 249 bags. How many packs do you have?

Elisa and Max look at each other and at the bundles. Nina suggests they count the packs. They count 24 packs in unison.

Nina: So you have 24 ...

Max: We have 24 packs.

Nina: Let's write that down. How many in each pack again?

Elisa: There's 10.

Nina: OK, 10 in each pack. There are 24 packs. And how many loose?

Elisa: There's 9 loose.

Max moves a pack of ten but counts by one instead of by ten as he crosses the centennial number 200—a common error when children learn to skip-count.

When Nina asks how many packs, Max replies with the number of bags, evidence that he is still developing place value.

The children do not know that the number of packs is embedded in the number 249; they need to count them.

Nina lets her voice trail off in order to see if the children are clear on what they are counting. She probes to check that they understand the meaning of all the numbers involved and then encourages them to record their findings.

continued on next page

continued from previous page

Nina: Do you see a place where the number of packs is in this number? *(Pointing to the number 249 on the paper.)*

Elisa: 24 and 9, and 24 and 9. Look!

Nina: So you mean 24 is the packs and the 9 is the loose? That's really interesting. Do you think if you counted something else with a big number that it would happen again?

Nina helps them notice the matching numerals in the written number that they might not have noticed on their own. Doing so encourages the children to become intrigued with place value patterns.

Nina pushes the children to consider whether the connection between the written number and the number of packs and loose bags is coincidental or whether they might be able to generalize about all numbers.

Preparing for the Math Congress

As the end of the workshop time nears, let children know that the class will gather on Day Four to share their findings. Today, children should spend time making sure of their counts and checking that their index cards include the names of the items, the total number of items, the number of packs, and the number of loose items. Remind the children to write their names on the back of the cards.

☀ Consider which numbers you will want to examine in the math congress on Day Four.

Tips for Structuring the Math Congress

As children finish their work, think about which numbers you will want to examine in the math congress on Day Four. Which number will you start with, and why? If making packs of ten is new for many children, it might be a good idea to start with a smaller number of items to count. Select a range of numbers that is appropriate for your group. Be sure to include some multiples of ten, which will provide an opportunity to discuss the role of zero in a number. Also, choose counts that include errors, or choose a pair of children who had difficulty in taking inventory to share. Results can be double-checked in the congress and errors can be examined.

Reflections on the Day

The minilesson today introduced the ten-frame—a helpful model to encourage the use of the five- and ten-structures. As the class continued packing and taking inventory, more children are beginning to skip-count and to count packs. Although place value understanding is not the immediate goal for all, it is appearing on the horizon for some.

DAY FOUR

Making the Class Inventory Chart

Materials Needed

Baskets of sorted objects and completed index cards from previous days

Large rubber bands, paper clips, and/or small bags to bundle materials

Children's work from Days One through Three

Chart of inventory data from Day Three

Markers

Children join in a math congress to gather and examine the inventory results they wrote on index cards on Day Three. They look for a pattern in the numbers and predict whether the pattern will occur with all numbers. Then they test their prediction as they continue inventory work.

Day Four Outline

Facilitating the Math Congress

☀ Use the chart made on Day Three to record children's findings.

☀ Discuss the pattern that appears in the numbers and whether children think the pattern will occur with all numbers.

Supporting the Investigation

☀ As children check their counts, ask them what they are thinking about the pattern in the numbers.

Preparing for the Math Congress

☀ Plan to focus the congress on children's inventory of math manipulatives so that larger numbers can be discussed.

Facilitating the Math Congress

Have children come to the math congress with their index cards. Have their baskets of items accessible nearby, in case they need to recheck their counts. Let the children know that they will be examining the data gathered for one type of item at a time. For example, ask children who have inventoried books to share their findings and record their results on chart paper; then move on to the next pair of children. Here a pair of children share their findings and add them to the chart that was started at the start of Day Three:

☀ Use the chart made on Day Three to record children's findings.

☀ Discuss the pattern that appears in the numbers and whether children think the pattern will occur with all numbers.

Item	How many in all?	How many packs of ten?	How many loose ones?
Basket A (small books)	13	1	3
Basket D (alphabet books)	34	3	4

If a count includes obvious errors—for example, if a child says, "We counted 29 books, so that's 3 packs and 0 loose"—ask the other children what they think. For example, you might say, "Kate said that the basket had 3 packs. How many books would that be? Who can check that count?" Do not emphasize the mistake; instead, consider it an opportunity to probe mathematical thinking and to encourage further reflection.

As you post the data, some children may start noticing a pattern in the numbers. Acknowledge but don't discuss the pattern with the entire class too soon—they need to see sufficient data to be able to describe the pattern with some confidence. If children point it out too soon, you might ask them to share with a neighbor; say, "Some of you may be noticing a pattern in the chart. Keep thinking about it, but let's hold off on discussing it together until we have more data—more numbers—up here to look at."

If no one mentions the pattern after seven or eight sets of numbers are posted, review the numbers, reading them aloud, and ask if anyone notices any pattern. Ask several children to describe the pattern, and wonder aloud whether it will always happen. Listen to what children say. If there seems to be a consensus that it will always work, wonder aloud why it occurs. Continue adding more results to the chart. Aim for a range of numbers, calling on children who counted small numbers of objects and children who counted large numbers of objects.

Expect that some children will make mistakes or get confused when they discuss the numbers of packs of ten, the number of loose items, and the total. Check regularly for understanding by asking children to clarify what they are counting when they talk about numbers. Expect also that children's understanding will be unsteady—they may seem to understand one moment but appear confused soon after.

It is one thing for children to identify a pattern and another thing for them to explain why the pattern occurs. Children might notice that, in the second column on the chart, the number on the right is the same as the number of loose items and that the number next to it on the left is the same as the number of packs. They may not, however, understand or be able to explain that the number of packs describes the number of tens. Remember that the process of constructing place value requires considerable time and experience.

Plan to spend about half an hour in this math congress, enough time to collect many sets of results, and to allow children to notice the pattern, so they can consider it as they continue to work with inventory counts. Explain that today children will revisit the items they have counted and check whether the pattern that was discussed occurs in each of their inventory counts. Tell them that they will examine the data in another math congress on Day Five, giving them additional opportunities to continue this discussion.

Inside One Classroom

A Portion of the Math Congress

Author's Notes

Nina (the teacher): Paula and David, what about your basket of books?

Paula: *(Reads the index card on the basket.)* There's 14 books—2 loose and 1 pack. Wait a minute—the pattern didn't happen again!

Previously the partners had noticed the place value pattern appearing on the chart, and now because of an error the pattern doesn't seem to hold.

Nina: Uh-oh.

David: It didn't do it again!

Keiko: Maybe it's 41.

Nina: Would that be OK? What do other people think? Talk to somebody next to you about this. Is this OK? *(Allows time for pair talk.)* What do you think?

Nina does not provide confirmation. Instead, she asks the community to consider the results.

Keiko: I don't think the pattern is going to happen again.

David: Maybe it *(pointing to the total)* should be 12 or maybe the loose things should be 4.

Paolo: It can't be like that. It's not possible.

Paolo's use of the term "not possible" shows his understanding of place value. Nina questions Paolo in order to focus the conversation on place value.

Nina: What's not possible?

Paolo: It's not possible to be like 14 and 2 and 1. One of those might be a mistake. This part *(points to the total of 14 on the chart)* might be a 12.

continued on next page

continued from previous page

Nina: If the total was 12, would that be OK then? Let's check it out. Here's the basket. *(Takes out a pack of books.)* I've got...a pack of books.

Paula: One pack.

Paolo: Let's see if they made a mistake in the pack.

Nina: Good idea. *(Counts the books in the pack; children count with her.)* There's 1, 2, 3, 4, 5, 6, 7, 8, 9, 10. *(Puts a rubber band back around the pack.)*

David: And 11, 12.

Nina: Right, 11, 12. How many loose ones are there?

David: Two.

Nina: Two loose. And how many packs?

Many voices: One.

Nina: And how many altogether?

Paula: Twelve.

Nina: So 12 altogether. *(Puts the information on the chart.)* And 1 pack and 2 loose ones. *(Puts the information on the chart)*.

Keiko: It did it again, it did it again! The pattern keeps happening!

> *Nina and the community explore incorrect answers as well as correct ones. Exploring incorrect answers can often result in powerful reflections.*

> *Mathematicians revel in patterns. For Keiko, though, this place value pattern is wondrous.*

Supporting the Investigation

Children will be leaving the congress with the guiding questions, "Will this pattern keep happening? Could we use this pattern to figure out how many packs and how many loose items there are, or if we already know how many packs and how many loose items, can the pattern help us figure out the total?" As children work, circulate among the pairs and see what they are working on.

✦ As they check their numbers, watch them pack and listen as they discuss their count. Are they clear about what they are counting? Ask questions to clarify and deepen understanding—for example, "You said 7. Is that 7 packs, or 7 books?"

✦ Ask children what they are thinking about the pattern. Some children will be convinced that the pattern always holds but don't understand why, while others will be able to say that the numeral on the right tells the number of loose and the numerals to the left of it describe the

> ☀ As children check their counts, ask them what they are thinking about the pattern in the numbers.

number of tens. You can challenge them to predict whether the pattern would hold if the packs contained five items instead of ten and whether it might work for packs of any other size.

Preparing for the Math Congress

☀ Plan to focus the congress on children's inventory of math manipulatives so that larger numbers can be discussed.

After confirming and correcting counts, children should take time to make sure that the numbers they have recorded on the index cards are accurate. Ask them to talk with their partners about what they think about the pattern in the numbers: did the pattern hold with their inventory counts or not? They should be prepared to share their thinking during the math congress on Day Five.

The congress on Day Five will center on math manipulatives and other materials which will be presented for counting in a range of large numbers. Plan for the congress by considering which numbers you will discuss, which pairs of children will share, and in which order. During today's investigation, did specific children or pairs change their minds about the pattern? Did some children have data that challenged the pattern? Did you want to share with the group an interesting idea on why the pattern will always hold? Which three-digit numbers will you want to offer for discussion?

Reflections on the Day

Children had many opportunities to make connections between the number of tens in a quantity and the numerals that represent the number. As they worked to construct a class chart of their results, they examined place value and investigated whether the pattern found would be present with all numbers.

Adding to the Class Inventory Chart

Children gather in the meeting area to share what they have noticed about the pattern in the numbers. They add to the chart of inventory data, exploring three-digit as well as two-digit numbers. Then they return to their inventory investigation with a new challenge: "What if we wanted only full packs of ten? How many more of each item would we need to order?"

Day Five Outline

Facilitating the Math Congress

☀ Have children share their results from the math manipulatives inventory and add that data to the chart from Day Four. Discuss whether the number pattern holds for three-digit numbers.

Developing the Context

☀ Explain that for today's investigation children will determine the numbers of each type of item that would need to be added so that their inventory would have no loose items.

Supporting the Investigation

☀ Note how children are figuring out how to get to the next multiple of ten and support them in using more efficient strategies.

Preparing for the Math Congress

☀ The math congress will be held on Day Six. Prepare to collect the data from today's investigation by adding new columns ("How many needed?" and "The new total") to the chart you have been using.

Materials Needed

Baskets of sorted objects and completed index cards from previous days

Large rubber bands, paper clips, and/or small bags to bundle materials

Chart of inventory data from Day Four

Sticky notes—one pad per pair of children

Markers

Facilitating the Math Congress

☀ Have children share their results from the math manipulatives inventory and add that data to the chart from Day Four. Discuss whether the number pattern holds for three-digit numbers.

Convene the children in the meeting area with partners sitting next to each other and inventory baskets accessible. You might want to start by asking one or two children to restate the pattern that the class was exploring on Day Four. Did the pattern work for any, some, or all numbers that they explored? If children offer any numbers that they say didn't fit the pattern, you might examine them together. Then move on to the inventory of math manipulatives. Ask several pairs, one at a time, to share their results. Add the numbers to the chart you made on Day Four. You might want to select a pair who struggled to describe their counts—was it the total number or the number of packs? Having to articulate their meaning often helps children clarify their own thinking.

These numbers will be greater than those discussed in the congress on Day Four, and should include more three-digit numbers. While some children might have worked with larger quantities already, today all children will be challenged to think about larger numbers. For a number like 137, some children will say the pattern doesn't hold because there are not 3 but rather 13 ten-packs, while others will argue that both digits to the left of the 7 describe the 13 packs. Be prepared with the materials to count the 13 packs by tens. It may be challenging for some children to count by tens beyond 100.

Inside One Classroom

A Portion of the Math Congress

Emi and Sharon took inventory of wooden craft sticks.

Emi: We counted 10 sticks and put rubber bands around them. Then we counted the packs, and we got 15 packs.

Sharon: And we had 7 sticks that didn't go into a pack, so that's 7 loose.

Nina (the teacher): Let's see. You counted 15 packs and 7 loose. How many sticks is that?

Emi and Sharon: It's 157.

Nina: Let's write that down—157 sticks, 15 packs, 7 loose.
(Records the numbers on the chart.)

Eddie: It didn't work this time.

Susanne: Maybe they counted wrong.

continued on next page

Author's Notes

Nina asks Emi and Sharon to share because there were more than 100 craft sticks—a three-digit number. She knows they have begun generalizing about two-digit numbers and wants to challenge their ideas of place value.

Without prompting, Eddie is already looking for patterns in the numbers.

continued from previous page

Nina: What didn't work? Can you explain what you are thinking, Eddie?

Eddie: It's 157 sticks. In the other numbers, the number next to the last one was the number of packs, like 17 was 1 pack and 7 loose, and 38 was 3 packs and 8 loose. If it worked there should be 5 packs, because the 5 is next to the 7, like in the other numbers.

Keiko: It did work!

(Many voices, some agreeing and some not.)

Nina: I'm hearing some of you say that the pattern happened here and some say it didn't. Eddie said why he thought it didn't happen. Let's hear some more thoughts on this.

Miguel: I agree with Keiko, because it's 15 packs and 7 loose.

Keiko: It works because it's OK if the number of packs has two numbers.

Nina: Does everyone agree that 157 has 15 packs of ten and 7 loose? If I unbundled one of these packs *(unbundles one as she speaks)*, do we still have 157? Turn to your partner and take turns sharing what you are thinking about this. *(After a few moments of pair talk, whole-group conversation resumes).* Miguel?

Miguel: It's still 157. It can be 15 packs and 7 loose or 14 packs and 17 loose. You didn't add any or take any away—you just opened a pack and made 'em loose.

Eddie: Yeah. I think you just have to make as many packs of 10 as you can to make the numbers match.

Eddie's current view of place value is limited to each digit. Many teachers focus their teaching of place value on the value of the column, so 157 would be described as 1 hundred, 5 tens, and 7 units. A narrow focus like this can lead to many problems. In contrast, Nina encourages the examination of 157 as 15 tens and 7 loose items. This amount is equivalent to 14 tens and 17 loose. Developing a strong sense of equivalence is critical as understanding of place value emerges.

Nina sees that several children are engaged in the question and invites other voices into the discussion.

Keiko means a number represented with two digits.

Nina hopes to involve as many children as possible. She listens in on their pair talk in order to assess their thinking and to decide whom to call on next.

Equivalence and place value are now the primary focus of the conversation.

Developing the Context

The inventory investigation now shifts to making full packs from any number. Explain how difficult it is to keep track of loose items in the baskets. Choose an item that has been inventoried and wonder aloud, "What if we wanted to add things to all the baskets so there were no loose items? This basket, for instance, has 13 books. How many books would I need to order to end up with only full packs and no loose books?"

Give children time to think about this and have them share their thinking with a neighbor. Listen to them as they talk. Do they count on from 13 to 20? Or do they use a familiar combination of ten, such as 3 + 7? Have one or two children share their thinking with the group. Write "7 more" on a sticky note and place it on the index card that was used for that basket.

☀ Explain that for today's investigation children will determine the numbers of each type of item that would need to be added so that their inventory would have no loose items.

Behind the Numbers

This investigation focuses on getting to the next multiple of ten. These numbers are often called "friendly numbers" because it is easy to add another number to them. Finding friendly numbers is an important strategy for adding numbers. When children can easily use combinations of ten to make another ten, they can add by chunks, moving away from counting on by ones. For instance, when solving 137 + 8, children can think about adding the 8 in two parts, to make 137 + 3 + 5. The plus 3 results in a landmark of 140. Adding 5 more is now easy.

☀ Note how children are figuring out how to get to the next multiple of ten and support them in using more efficient strategies.

Ask the children to help you determine the numbers of each type of item to order so that their inventory would have no loose items. Have them return to the baskets they inventoried and record on sticky notes the number of items needed to make full packs with no loose items. They should attach these sticky notes to the index cards they used for each basket of items.

Supporting the Investigation

As children work, circulate around the room and take notes on how they are figuring out how to get to the next multiple of ten. Here are some ways you can support their thinking:

✦ Are they counting the items themselves to figure how many they need, or do they start by looking at the numbers on the index cards and using what they know about place value? If they are not using the numbers, guide their attention to the index cards. You might ask, "What do you know already by looking at these numbers? Can any of those numbers help you figure out how many more you need?"

✦ Are they counting on by ones? You can support these children by giving them friendly numbers like 25 and seeing if they can move from counting by ones to jumping a five. If they can, have them work on another basket of items and challenge them to see if they can figure out how many items there are without counting each one.

✦ Are they using five as a landmark? If they're starting with 34 items, perhaps they know that it's one more to 35 and then 5 more to 40, so they would need 6 more. Using the five-structure is a great way for children to learn combinations that make ten.

✦ Do they use combinations that make ten? Note which children know the combinations that make ten and which children don't. These children may benefit from games (one will be introduced on Day Six) that help them learn combinations of whole numbers that make ten.

✦ Do they ignore the ten-packs and just consider the number of loose items? You can ask children, before they start counting, to predict how many they might need and how they know. Sometimes children start counting even though they might know more efficient methods. Considering the number before they start counting might help them use strategies in a deliberate way.

Differentiating Instruction

Some children might already know combinations of ten and jump quickly to the next multiple of ten. You might challenge these children by asking them to predict which other numbers would make only ten-packs (with no loose items), or how many they would need to get to other landmarks such as 50 or 100.

Preparing for the Math Congress

As the end of math workshop nears, tell the children that they will be sharing their work during the math congress on Day Six, so they should check their numbers and make sure they are legible. You can have them bring the index cards (with the sticky notes) to the congress on Day Six.

Prepare to collect the data by adding new columns to the chart you have been using, or you can tape a new chart over the old, leaving exposed the column with the original inventory totals. Label the new columns "How many needed?" and "The new total."

☀ The math congress will be held on Day Six. Prepare to collect the data from today's investigation by adding new columns ("How many needed?" and "The new total") to the chart you have been using.

Reflections on the Day

Children have begun to think about how many more of an item are needed to get to the next multiple of ten. This helps them to think further about the place value patterns and prepares them for adding numbers. An important strategy for addition is keeping one addend whole—i.e., not decomposing it into tens and ones—and decomposing the other addend, a strategy that makes use of decade landmarks. The work children started today will help to develop this strategy.

DAY SIX

Recording the Orders for Full Packs and Playing Rolling for Tens

Materials Needed

Chart of inventory data from Day Five (or start a new chart)

Completed index cards (with attached sticky notes) from Day Five

Drawing paper—a few sheets per group of three or four children

Set of 20 number cubes (with numbers or dots, one through six) in a plastic bag—one set per group of three or four children

Ten-frames *(optional)*

Markers

At the math congress, children share the data they collected on Day Five, giving the number of items needed to complete full packs. The game Rolling for Tens is then introduced and children play it in groups of three or four.

Day Six Outline

Facilitating the Math Congress

☀ Record the data from the investigation on Day Five and ask children if they notice any new patterns in the numbers.

Developing the Context

☀ Model how to play Rolling for Tens.

Supporting the Investigation

☀ Note children's strategies for computing combinations of ten.

Facilitating the Math Congress

Children gather in the meeting area with the data they collected on Day Five. Invite some children to share their numbers and post them on the chart. Ask them to explain how they got the number (e.g., counting on by ones or using combinations of ten). You can use ten-frames to model their thinking.

After a number of children have shared, ask if anyone notices any new patterns on the chart. Here are some things that children may notice:

☀ Record the data from the investigation on Day Five and ask children if they notice any new patterns in the numbers.

✦ The number of packs increases by one. (This can be checked, if you started a new chart, by exposing the "How many packs of ten?" column on the previous chart.) Or, closely related, the number of tens increases by one. Some children may not see these two ideas as the same concept.

✦ The number in the ones place plus the number that is needed to make a full pack always equals ten.

✦ All the loose items are now recorded as zero and the new totals all end in zero.

As patterns emerge, have children paraphrase the ideas expressed, and ask why the patterns occur. Listen for evidence of understanding—or confusion—about place value.

Developing the Context

Discuss how some children used combinations of ten to figure out how many items they needed to make full packs. Because those combinations are so helpful when adding numbers, explain that you are going to introduce a game that will help the class learn and practice ways to make ten. Have the children sit in a circle, and choose a partner to play the game with you as you introduce Rolling for Tens.

☀ Model how to play Rolling for Tens.

▨ Object of the Game

The purpose of Rolling for Tens is to learn and develop fluency with combinations of ten, using two or more addends. Automatizing the combinations that sum to ten is a critical step that will allow children to easily find the next multiple of ten when adding numbers.

▨ Directions for Playing Rolling for Tens

Children play the game in groups of three or four. One player sets up the game by emptying the plastic bag of number cubes onto the table. Players take turns selecting two or more cubes that add up to ten, and justifying their selections. Play continues until no more combinations of ten are possible. The total of the dots or numbers on the remaining cubes is recorded as a score. For example, if three cubes (2, 4, 3) remain as unusable, the score for that round is recorded as 9. Children record the combinations on blank paper and then place the cubes used back in the bag. Five rounds are played in total and players work together to achieve the lowest total score possible.

Supporting the Investigation

☀ Note children's strategies for computing combinations of ten.

As children play the game, watch how they compute combinations of ten. Which children know the combinations already? Most children will know 5 + 5 already and perhaps 6 + 4. How do they add three or more cubes to make ten? For instance, with cubes numbered 2, 2, and 6, do they start with the six, the largest number, and add two and then two more? Do they combine the 2 + 2 to make the familiar combination 6 + 4? If working with cubes that have dots, do children count each dot, or do they subitize (know the number of dots at a glance) and count on?

Differentiating Instruction

Do some children routinely count every dot starting from one? You might substitute cubes with numerals (instead of dots) to encourage these children to count on. This is one of many games that develop fluency with combinations of ten. The *Contexts for Learning Mathematics* resource unit *Games for Early Number Sense* contains many other games that the class can play in place of or in addition to Rolling for Tens.

Reflections on the Day

Today children had several opportunities to work on combinations of addends that sum to ten. They also continued to explore place value as they determined the number of items needed to complete their inventories (making full packs of ten) and as they examined patterns in the numbers.

Making Packs of Five

Children are introduced to a new investigation involving taking inventory: packing items in sets of five rather than ten. They collect data on baskets of sorted items and share their findings.

Day Seven Outline

Developing the Context

☀ Explain that today children will investigate what happens when they change packs of ten to packs of five.

Supporting the Investigation

☀ Note children's strategies as they repack materials.

Preparing for the Math Congress

☀ Prepare a new chart that lists the total number of items, the number of packs of ten and of loose items, and the number of packs of five and of loose items.

Facilitating the Math Congress

☀ Record children's findings on the new chart and discuss the patterns in the numbers.

☀ Discuss whether the numbers of ten-packs can be used to figure out the number of five-packs.

☀ Talk about whether there is a way to determine how many five-packs there will be without needing to repack.

Materials Needed

Baskets of sorted objects and completed index cards from previous days

Student recording sheet for making fives (Appendix C)—one per pair of children

Drawing paper—a few sheets per pair of children

Clipboards—one per pair of children

Large chart pad and easel

Markers

Developing the Context

☀ Explain that today children will investigate what happens when they change packs of ten to packs of five.

Appendix C — Student recording sheet for making fives

Children's understanding of place value is challenged and deepened today by having them investigate groups of five items instead of ten. You can introduce the new packing format by noticing aloud that some large items—such as books, wooden blocks, or dry-erase boards—were difficult to bundle in packs of ten and that even after the inventory it is still difficult to notice when such items are missing. It occurred to you that smaller packs of five might be better. Ask, "What would happen if we changed the packs of ten to packs of five?" You might ask some children to share their conjectures. Do they consider what will happen to the pattern? Do they predict that the number of packs will increase, or that they will double? What will happen to the loose items?

Use this discussion as a way to assess children's mathematical thinking. Don't take the time now to investigate or try to respond to any of their predictions. Allow the wonderings to arise—you can record them if you want to—so children can think about them as they work. Then send the children off with blank paper to work out their thinking (they may find it helpful to draw). Have them record their findings on the recording sheet (Appendix C).

Behind the Numbers

The relationship between the five- and the ten-structures is important because it underlies a deep understanding of our number system. Encourage children to notice that every pack of ten makes two packs of five and that the loose items may be regrouped as well. Six, for instance, can be regrouped into a five and a one. Often children assume that the number of packs will just double, but this is not the case, since the loose items, when regrouped into new packs of five, might increase the number of packs.

The five-structure, as it utilizes the human trait of subitizing—recognizing small units like one, two and three without needing to count—is helpful in automatizing the basic facts. Many researchers believe that this ability is innate. The five-structure builds on this ability. Seven, for example, when thought of as 5 and 2, is easily seen as needing 3 to make another 5 (and thus 7 + 3 is equivalent to 10). Regrouping the loose items when the amount is larger than five is important to provide children with concrete, hands-on opportunities to develop an understanding of these relationships.

Supporting the Investigation

As children work, take note of their strategies and support their mathematical thinking with guiding questions as they talk among themselves. Encourage them to repack as a way to double-check and to keep the context authentic. If any items have been misplaced over the last week, children may be surprised to discover that their predictions don't match and then they will need to recheck the groups of ten. This rechecking of tens is important too, as the heart of this investigation is the relationship between the five- and the ten-structure. As you move around and confer, notice the children's strategies:

✦ Do children repack all the materials and recount starting from one? Do they count each pack of ten twice, or count by twos?

✦ Do children just count and record, or do they independently notice the place value patterns in the numbers? For instance, do they notice that the number of packs either doubles or is double plus one? Some children need prompting to think about the numbers, but wait until they have gathered several sets of data before asking them what they are noticing.

☀ Note children's strategies as they repack materials.

- Do children think that the number of groups will just double and are they surprised to discover that this is not always the case? What do they think will happen with the loose items? Can they make a general statement that will allow them to work with the numbers on the index cards, using the number of ten-packs to figure out the number of five-packs?

Preparing for the Math Congress

Let the children know that in the math congress you will be making a new chart to post the new results. Ask them to be prepared to share the total number of items, the number of packs of five they made, and the number of loose items remaining. Have them record their results and bring their recording sheets to the congress.

☀ Prepare a new chart that lists the total number of items, the number of packs of ten and of loose items, and the number of packs of five and of loose items.

Facilitating the Math Congress

Plan on starting the congress by making a chart for the new results. The new chart should list the total number of items, the number of packs of ten and of loose items, and then the number of packs of five and of loose items. You will want to get the results up on the chart fairly quickly so the congress can focus on a few questions:

- Could the numbers on the index cards used to label baskets for packs of ten be used to figure out the number of packs of five and the number of loose items?

- If the total number of items is known, is there a way to figure out how many packs of five there will be without needing to repack?

- Do any patterns appear in this new data?

Ask children, one pair at a time, to share their numbers. As you add the numbers to the chart, ask the class to confirm that the numbers are accurate. Be sure that enough sets of results—at least six or eight sets of numbers—are posted before discussing patterns. Then ask children to share what they have noticed. If no one specifically brings it up, ask them whether the same pattern that occurred with the tens occurred again with the fives. When children answer no, ask why not. How does the number of packs of five compare to the number of packs when they made groups of ten? In turn, examine the three questions listed above.

☀ Record children's findings on the new chart and discuss the patterns in the numbers.

☀ Discuss whether the numbers of ten-packs can be used to figure out the number of five-packs.

☀ Talk about whether there is a way to determine how many five-packs there will be without needing to repack.

A Portion of the Math Congress

Nina (the teacher): So you've noticed some interesting patterns here. Keiko said there were never a lot of loose items…just 1, 2, 3, or 4. And Eddie noticed that every pack of 10 had two packs of 5. I wonder what is going on here. Do you think there is any way we could use our old inventory with packs of ten to figure out this new inventory with packs of five? Zoë?

Zoë: I think the packs will just be double…because there's 2 fives in every ten…like Eddie said.

Nina: How many people agree with Zoë? Thumbs-up if you agree; thumbs-down if you don't…and wiggle it if you're not sure. *(Notes that most thumbs are up, a few down, and a few wiggling.)* Emi, your thumb was down. Tell us what you are thinking.

Emi: Sharon and I did the inventory of the pencils. There were 36. We had 3 packs of tens and 6 loose. When we made packs of five we had 7 and just 1 loose.

Eddie: That's weird.

Nina: Let's check it out. Bring the pencil basket over, Emi. *(Together they check out the total number if pencils are bundled in packs of ten, and then with packs of five.)*

Eddie: Oh, yeah. There's a 5 in the 6. We can make another pack of 5. Hey…maybe that's why the loose ones are always little amounts. They have to be 1, 2, 3, or 4. If they're 5, they make another pack.

Nina: How many people can put in their own words what Eddie is proposing as a conjecture?

Author's Notes

Nina shifts the conversation to the heart of the matter: Can knowing the number of packs of ten help us to know how many fives? The relationship between the five- and the ten-structure will now be examined. For instance, the children might realize that a multiple of ten is always a multiple of five.

By asking for a choice of three options Nina ensures that everyone must think about this and commit one way or the other. No one can stay disengaged.

Mathematicians raise conjectures and then work to prove them. Nina supports her young mathematicians in this process.

Reflections on the Day

Today children worked further with the five- and the ten-structures of our number system. Thinking about the loose items with the five-structure will support them as they automatize the combinations of addends that make ten. These concepts are critical, and the children are developing many ways of envisioning number as they compose, decompose, pack, and determine the numbers of items needed to make full packs. They are discussing patterns in our place value system as well as attributes of our number system in general. For instance, they might notice that a multiple of ten is always a multiple of five, or that the number of loose ones is always less than ten when packing in groups of ten, and is always less than five when packing in groups of five.

DAY EIGHT

Collecting Stamps

A new game, Collecting Stamps, is introduced today to foster children's understanding of ten as both ten items, and as one group. After children pair up and play the game, they meet in a brief math congress to share and discuss strategies they found helpful.

Day Eight Outline

Developing the Context

☀ Model how to play Collecting Stamps.

Supporting the Investigation

☀ Note children's strategies as they play the game.

Preparing for the Math Congress

☀ Plan to focus the congress on important addition strategies such as using landmark numbers and taking jumps of ten.

Facilitating the Math Congress

☀ Tell a stamp story using the game context as a way to elicit children's strategies.

☀ Discuss how some strategies are more efficient than others.

Materials Needed

Collecting Stamps game board and game pieces (Appendix D)—one set per pair of children

Number cubes (with numbers or dots, one through six)—two per pair of children

Number cards *(optional)* **(Appendix E)**—one set per pair of children

Drawing paper and markers, as needed

Developing the Context

☀ Model how to play Collecting Stamps.

Remind the children of the inventory work they have done so far—deciding how many ten-packs and loose items may be made from the total, figuring how many items to add to the loose ones to make full packs of ten, and repeating the process for packs of five. Bring up the strategies they have developed. Tell them they will be using what they have learned as they play a new game, Collecting Stamps.

Have children sit in a circle to learn the game. (The game can also be introduced using an overhead projector, with transparent game pieces.) Choose a child to be your game partner as you model how to play.

▦ Object of the Game

The purpose of the game is to collect 100 stamps, filling ten pages of an empty stamp book (the game board). The game supports the making of ten as an addition strategy, and the unitizing of a group of ten. The stamp pages on the game board are designed to resemble ten-frames to support the use of the five- and ten-structures as helpful models.

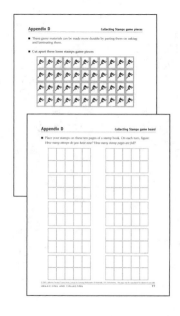

▦ Directions for Playing Collecting Stamps

Children are paired up, with one game board, a set of stamps, a set of Full Page game pieces (Appendix D), and a pair of number cubes. Players take turns tossing the number cubes and collecting stamps. The number of stamps collected and placed on the board is the sum of the numbers tossed. Whenever ten stamps are collected, they are exchanged for a Full Page game piece. After each toss, players state how many stamps they have collected and how many stamp pages have been filled. The game is over when 100 or more stamps have been collected.

Supporting the Investigation

☀ Note children's strategies as they play the game.

As the children play the game, circulate among the pairs and take note of their mathematical thinking.

✦ How are children adding the two numbers on the number cubes? Are they counting dots, counting on from one cube to the next, or do they just know the combinations? If children are counting each dot, consider using one cube with numerals and one cube with dots to encourage counting on.

✦ If children roll more than 10 on a single roll, do they collect individual stamps or do they realize immediately that they are eligible for a Full Page game piece?

✦ How do children collect the stamps? For example, if 2 stamps are on a page and a child rolls 9, does the child add 8 stamps to the 2 already there, or does the child remove one of the 2 stamps and just take a Full Page game piece?

✦ How do children figure out the total number of stamps? Do they count by groups of ten or one by one? How do they skip-count? Are they unitizing, knowing that four full pages (4 tens) are also 40 stamps?

Differentiating Instruction

Some children may benefit from recording the equation that reflects their move—for example, $34 + 9 = 43$. You can help children think about the way they got the 43: "So first you added 6 to the 34 to get 40, and then you added 3 more to get 43." Children who are ready to work with numbers over 100 can use two or three game boards to collect 200 or 300 stamps. Variations of the game are possible as well. For example, instead of collecting 100 stamps, children practice laying out quantities of stamps using the number cards in Appendix E. (The numbers range from 4 to 100 in set #1 and from 102 to 250 in set #2.) Do children know that 46 stamps equal 4 full pages and 6 loose stamps, or do they count them out? How do they count out 120 stamps?

▩ Assessment Tips

As children play the game repeatedly, you can observe and note if their strategies change over time. You may want to photocopy the landscape of learning graphic (page 10) and, for each child, shade in the landmarks as you find evidence in their work. In a sense, you will be mapping the developmental journey of each of your budding mathematicians.

Appendix E			Number Cards
		Set #2	
102	109	110	114
115	120	128	131
137	146	149	151
155	162	166	173

Appendix E			Number cards
		Set #1	
4	9	10	13
16	18	20	22
26	27	31	33
39	40	43	46
48	51	56	57
62	65	69	70
73	78	82	85
87	90	98	100

Preparing for the Math Congress

After children have played the game once or twice, tell them that the class will be meeting to discuss addition strategies they found helpful as they played. Ask them to discuss with their partners a strategy or two to share.

☀ Plan to focus the congress on important addition strategies such as using landmark numbers and taking jumps of ten.

▩ Tips for Structuring the Math Congress

Note if children are using the stamp pages on the game board as ten-frames. This is an important approach to discuss because it leads to an addition strategy described in the overview—starting with one addend and decomposing the other to move to a landmark decade. For example, if a player has 24 stamps (2 full stamp pages and 4 loose) and the roll is a 4 and a 3, does he know that he will fill the 6 empty spaces on the stamp page (and exchange for a Full Page game piece) and one additional stamp? Other children, in calculating tosses that add up to more than ten, may take a Full Page game piece immediately. This is also a useful method to discuss as it leads to another important addition strategy—taking jumps of ten.

Facilitating the Math Congress

☀ Tell a stamp story using the game context as a way to elicit children's strategies.

☀ Discuss how some strategies are more efficient than others.

Have children gather at the edge of the meeting area around a game board (or you can use overhead transparencies of the game materials). Write a problem on the board and tell a stamp story using the game context. For example, 26 + 11:"I had 26 stamps and then I tossed a 5 and a 6, so I can put 11 more stamps on my game board. How many do I have now?"Ask a child to help place 26 stamps (commenting on her strategy if she uses 2 Full Page game pieces and 6 loose stamps), and then ask for different ways to add the 11. Use the game pieces to illustrate the strategies that children suggest. Here are some possible strategies:

Counting on 11 from 26

26 + 4 = 30, 30 + 7 = 37

26 + 10 = 36, 36 + 1 = 37

In discussing each strategy, emphasize that while counting on works, the latter two strategies are more efficient.

Reflections on the Day

In the game Collecting Stamps, children worked with models of ten-frames to add numbers. Helpful strategies for addition were discussed in the math congress, for instance, jumping to the next multiple of ten, or adding ten to a number.

Completing the Inventory with New Orders

The day begins with a minilesson using quick images of ten-frames. Returning to their inventory, children investigate what happens when new orders (complete packs of ten) are added to baskets, and they share their findings in a math congress.

Day Nine Outline

Minilesson: Quick Images

☀ Display a string of quick images using ten-frames. The minilesson is designed to build on the place value pattern children explored during their inventory work.

Developing the Context

☀ Explain that today children will investigate what happens when new orders of materials, this time in complete packs of ten, are added to their baskets.

Supporting the Investigation

☀ Note the addition strategies children use and encourage them to recognize the patterns that occur when they add 10 to a number.

Preparing for the Math Congress

☀ Plan to focus the math congress on the patterns children have been exploring.

Facilitating the Math Congress

☀ As children share their results, discuss whether the numbers fit the place value patterns they have been exploring.

☀ Focus the discussion on equivalence and the increasing amounts of ten.

Materials Needed

Ten-frames (Appendix B)

Before class, prepare overhead transparencies of the ten-frames listed in the string on page 50 (or you can display enlarged photocopies of the ten-frames).

Overhead projector (optional)

Baskets of sorted items and completed index cards from previous days

Sticky notes—one pad per pair of children

Chart of inventory data from Day Six

5" x 8" index cards—one per pair of children

Ten-frames—some full and some blank (enough for the largest number you might want to discuss during the math congress; see pages 52–53.)

Large chart pad and easel

Markers

Minilesson: Quick Images (10–15 minutes)

☀ Display a string of quick images using ten-frames. The minilesson is designed to build on the place value pattern children explored during their inventory work.

This minilesson uses a series of quick images with several ten-frames at once (Appendix B). It builds on the pattern that children have explored during their inventory work, in that 2 filled ten-frames are made up of 20 dots, 4 filled ten-frames have 40 dots, etc. Show each quick image for about five seconds, long enough to allow children to see groups and to know the ten-frame is full, but not long enough for children to count each dot. Ask them to tell their neighbor how many dots there are and how they know, and invite a few children to share with the whole group.

Behind the Numbers

The first image reminds children that a full frame contains 10 dots and that half a frame is 5 dots. The next two images, 20 and 22, require children to consider 2 tens as 20 and then to add 2. The last two images invite children to mentally manipulate the images to complete the ten-frames, or to envision full ten-frames with a few blanks.

String of related quick images:

15: shown as 10 + 5 dots

20: shown as 10 + 10 dots

22: shown as 10 + 10 + 2 dots

23: shown as 10 + 5 + 8 (shown as 5 + 3) dots

28: shown as 10 + 9 + 9

Developing the Context

☀ Explain that today children will investigate what happens when new orders of materials, this time in complete packs of ten, are added to their baskets.

Explain that although the class produced a wonderful list of the needed loose items on Day Six, you found that often (depending on the materials) it was difficult to order small numbers of loose items. For example, many of the items (like connecting cubes or markers) come in packs. You might show the class a few catalogs for office supplies or for math manipulatives as a way to authenticate the context. Next, pull out one of the previously inventoried baskets—for example, connecting cubes or markers—and look at the total number of items listed on the index card. Share it aloud (or read it off of the class chart from Day Six). For example, you might say, "We had 132 markers. It wasn't possible for me to order just 8 markers, but I can order a pack of 10. If I do, how many will we have?" Allow think time; then ask a few children to share their thinking. They might use the following strategies:

+ Counting on by ones from 132

+ Making leaps of ten using knowledge of place value: the 13 packs become 14 packs, then plus 2

+ Decomposing one addend and moving to a landmark decade:
  $132 + 10 = 132 + 8 + 2 = 140 + 2 = 142$

+ Splitting using partial sums:
  $132 + 10 = 130 + 2 + 10 = 140 + 2 = 142$

A few children may still be surprised that there is a 2 in both 132 and 142 and that the 13 increased to 14. Some may no longer be surprised but may still think this is coincidental, while others may now have a solid understanding of place value and be able to predict and use the place value patterns. In today's investigation, children will have the opportunity to explore addition further. This conversation is just a way to launch their thinking.

Then wonder aloud, "A few days ago we figured out how many items we would need to make only complete packs of ten." Refer to the class chart of inventory data that you made on Day Six. "Just now we didn't make complete packs but instead we added a whole pack. What if this happened with all our baskets? What if we could add more packs of ten things to every basket?" Tell the children that today they will be helping to figure out the results of new orders, if full ten-packs of items are delivered. You can have the children record the number on sticky notes, perhaps using a different color than they used for recording the numbers that would complete packs of ten. For example,

Markers + 10	
28	38

Send them off with their partners to investigate the results of the new orders.

Differentiating Instruction

Although this new investigation—jumping by ten—is introduced to the entire class, adding ten may be easy for many children, so at this point in the unit it is appropriate and important for children to be working on different kinds of inventory tasks. For this investigation you can introduce a variety of numbers to add as incoming orders. Some children may be challenged by the task of counting on ten more, especially if they do not have physical objects to count. Others can be adding much larger numbers, for example, adding 50 cubes to 132 cubes. Don't be afraid to challenge children with orders like 40, or 60, or 100. You might photocopy some pages from catalogs or allow children to look through them. Most items come in a variety of sizes and will provide nice multiples of ten to challenge children with. Children who understand why the tens digit increases when they add 10 can explore large, three-digit numbers, or they can add multiples of ten, such as +20, +30, +40. What happens when numbers cross the centennial, for example, 184 + 30? You might ask children who are working on the same investigation to sit together at the same table, where they can watch and help each other and where you can confer with more than one pair at a time if you see common struggles.

Supporting the Investigation

☀ Note the addition strategies children use and encourage them to recognize the patterns that occur when they add 10 to a number.

As children work, watch how they are adding and take note of what strategies they are using.

✦ Do they use a pack of ten or their fingers to count on by ones? Do they add by getting to a multiple of ten? After they have found results for two or more new orders, ask them to look at their numbers and see if they notice any patterns in the numbers when they add 10 to a number. Ask if they can predict what their next +10 number will be, and then allow them to check and confirm using any strategy they are comfortable with.

✦ Do they already know what the +10 sum will be? Ask questions to probe the depth of their understanding: "How did you know that so quickly, without counting?" "Why do you think that works?" "Can you show me with the cubes in this basket what the 5 in 57 means?" If they can explain clearly that the 5 refers to 5 tens, challenge them with bigger numbers, between 80 and 250. "Will the pattern work with any number? What about 126? What do you think you will have if you add 10 to 126?" Children who easily add 10 to two-digit numbers may guess that 126 + 10 = 226, assuming that the number "on the left" increases by one.

Preparing for the Math Congress

☀ Plan to focus the math congress on the patterns children have been exploring.

After children have added 10 (or multiples of 10) to at least three different numbers, announce a math congress to share what they've learned about the pattern they've been exploring. Ask children to copy all their counts (original and +10) on one index card to bring to the congress, so they can leave their sticky notes on the index cards they filled out on prior days. Depending on what the children were discussing, you might want to ask specific children to share their findings. Prepare a large chart to collect the data. You might also want to prepare ten-frames to model children's thinking during the math congress.

Facilitating the Math Congress

☀ As children share their results, discuss whether the numbers fit the place value patterns they have been exploring.

☀ Focus the discussion on equivalence and the increasing amounts of ten.

Gather children in the meeting area with their data. Ask pairs of children to share one set of numbers at a time, and record the numbers on the chart you have prepared. Have them model, with ten-frames or with items from the baskets, how they figured the new result. For instance,

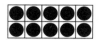

When the community has agreed that the numbers are correct, ask whether these numbers fit the place value pattern they have been exploring. Be sure that children explicitly discuss how the number of packs is increasing by one each time and that this result is reflected in the digits to the left of the units. Do not focus on the tens column. It is important that the focus be on equivalence and the increasing amounts of ten. For example, in considering the marker order discussed earlier today, help children remember the discussion in the prior week that 132 is 13 packs of ten and 2 loose items. And now another pack has been added. If your students can handle the challenge, ask them to consider adding 8 packs (an order of 80 new items) to a number like 132 (so the sum crosses the next hundred). Encourage them to consider this as 13 packs plus 8 packs for a total of 21 packs and 2 loose items, or 212. Working this way with place value, rather than isolating numbers into columns, builds deep number sense. If any children come up with incorrect numbers, ask them to share and allow them to discover and correct their own errors as they explain their thinking.

Reflections on the Day

Children had opportunities today to explore how helpful place value patterns can be when adding multiples of ten. At this point, different children may be at very different places in their development of an understanding of number. Still, no matter where they are on the landscape of learning, they are all being challenged and they are all acquiring insight into place value.

Games

Materials Needed

Ten-frames (Appendix B)

Before class, prepare overhead transparencies of the ten-frames listed in the string on page 55 (or you can display enlarged photocopies of the ten-frames).

Overhead projector *(optional)*

Collecting Stamps game board and game pieces from Day Eight—one set per pair of children

Number cards (Appendix E)—one set per pair of children

Student recording sheet for Collecting Stamps (Appendix F)—one per pair of children

Number cubes (with numbers or dots, one through six)—two per pair of children

Multiples-of-ten cubes (number cubes labeled +10, +10, +10, +20, +20, +30)—one per pair of children

Markers

Today's math workshop opens with a minilesson of quick images that focuses on adding 10 to a number. Children then pair up to revisit the game Collecting Stamps, but with an added twist.

Day Ten Outline

Minilesson: Quick Images

☀ Display a series of quick images focused on adding 10 to a number.

Games

☀ Decide which games children will play based on the specific mathematical ideas they are working on.

Supporting the Investigation

☀ As children play the games, listen for evidence of their thinking, their strategies, and their misconceptions.

Minilesson: Quick Images (10–15 minutes)

This minilesson is a string of related quick images (Appendix B). These problems focus on adding 10 to a number, supporting the +10 pattern that was introduced and explored on Day Nine. Show each quick image for about five seconds, long enough to allow children to see groups, and ask them how many dots they saw. Ask them to share their thinking with a neighbor, and invite a few children to share with the whole group.

☀ Display a series of quick images focused on adding 10 to a number.

String of related quick images:

24: shown as 10 + 10 + 4 dots

34: shown as 10 + 10 + 10 + 4 dots

47: shown as (10 + 10) + (10 + 10) + 5 + 2 dots

57: shown as (10 + 10 + 10) + (10 + 10) + 5 + 2 dots

25: shown as 10 + 10 + 5 dots

45: shown as (10 + 10) + (10 + 10) + 5 dots

Behind the Numbers

The numbers in this minilesson have been carefully chosen to support unitizing the ten as a group. The amounts of tens are shown in small groups of two or three to allow them to be subitized—seen as a group with just a glance. Children have to use this information to determine the total number of dots. The first two pairs are related to each other by an additional ten-frame. The last two are related by adding two tens. For the third and fourth problems, be sure that you place the ten-frames together in small groups, as shown by the parentheses, to allow for subitizing.

Games

After the minilesson, the children will begin playing the games. Everyone has already learned and played the game Collecting Stamps. Today several variations can be offered:

☀ Decide which games children will play based on the specific mathematical ideas they are working on.

+ Collecting Stamps (Original version)
+ Collecting Stamps with Number Cards (Variation 1)
+ Collecting Stamps with Multiples-of-Ten Cube (Variation 2)

▨ Collecting Stamps (Original version)

The original Collecting Stamps game is described on page 46. It is helpful for children to record their moves today, using the recording sheet (Appendix F). After each turn, the player should write a number sentence that indicates how many stamps were added and the new total. For example, if a player had 5 stamps and collected 6 more, the recording would be 5 + 6 = 11.

▨ Collecting Stamps with Number Cards (Variation 1)

Instead of collecting 100 stamps, children lay out quantities of stamps based on the number cards chosen (Appendix E). The numbers range from 4 to 100 in one set of numbers, and from 102 to 250 in another set.

■ Collecting Stamps with Multiples-of-Ten Cube (Variation 2)

The game is played with the same rules as the original Collecting Stamps (played on Day Eight), but one of the number cubes is replaced by a multiples-of-ten cube. This means that on each turn the player will add a quantity ranging from 11 to 36. (The multiples-of-ten cube is marked +10 on three sides and +20, +20, +30, on the other three.)

Differentiating Instruction

When determining which games children should play, consider the mathematics that they are working on. All the games build important concepts and strategies related to place value, but they vary in their emphasis. The numbers increase by smaller increments in the original version of Collecting Stamps. This game supports children who tend to count on by ones and who are working on the strategy of jumping to multiples of ten. The version with the number cards (Variation 1) supports children as they develop connections between the total number and the equivalent number of tens and ones. When Collecting Stamps is played with one number cube and one multiples-of-ten cube (Variation 2), the game challenges children to add larger numbers that are not multiples of ten.

Supporting the Investigation

☀ As children play the games, listen for evidence of their thinking, their strategies, and their misconceptions.

As children play the games, circulate among them and listen for evidence of their thinking, their strategies, and their misconceptions. What is their understanding of place value? Are they clear on the total number and the number of groups? Do they use multiples of ten (friendly numbers) as landmarks in computation? Do they comfortably add ten or multiples of ten to a number?

■ Assessment Tips

Keep a checklist of the games that each child is playing, and take notes on the strategies the child is using. You might note on the checklist whether the children are ready to move on to a different variation, or whether they need more time with a specific game. The next time you offer the games, you can form groups of children with similar needs. Continue to examine the graphic of the landscape of learning. Where is each child on the landscape, now that this unit is ending? What is still on the horizon?

Reflections on the Unit

A child's conceptual growth in understanding our number system parallels the historical development of number systems. The mathematician Hermann Weyl once said, "Numbers have neither substance, nor meaning, nor qualities. They are nothing but marks, and all that is in them we have put into them by the simple rule of straight succession." (Weyl 1959) Just as human beings put quantitative meaning into symbols over time, children's symbol usage as they work to record amounts and keep track progresses from tallies to groups to numerals—from additive systems to multiplicative systems (Fosnot and Dolk 2001).

Unitizing a group of ten is a big idea underlying place value. Critical addition strategies relating to place value are adding amounts to get to the next decade landmark, and taking leaps of ten. All these ideas and strategies were explored in this unit within the context of taking inventory of the materials in the classroom as children were invited to find ways to mathematize situations in their own "lived worlds." Since it took humans so long to construct a number system based on place value, how can we not be impressed with the seriousness of young children's mathematical endeavors, their struggles to invent such big ideas, and their capacity to mathematize?

Up a big, big hill, down a long, long path, through a thick, thick forest, there is an old, old house. This is the house of Nicholas Masloppy.

Nicholas is six years old and he loves his big, old house. There are lots and lots and lots of rooms. Once he even got lost in his own house!

Nicholas lives there with his Uncle Lloyd . . . .

his Grandma Eudora . . .

his sisters Henrietta, Delia, Violet, and Petula . . .

his baby brother, Oscar . . .

and his dog, Itchy.

Nicholas loves his family. Everybody looks out for each other, everybody is helpful, and everybody always shares. The only problem is that the house is so big, and his family is so large, that whenever Nicholas needs something he can't find it! Like the time he took home his library book from school and his teacher asked him the following week to bring it back. Nicholas wanted to return the book, but he couldn't find it. He looked and looked. His sister, Henrietta, had borrowed it from him. When he asked Henrietta where it was, she didn't know because Violet had borrowed it from her. Nicholas kept looking. Uncle Lloyd had borrowed it from Violet, and Grandma Eudora had borrowed it from him. Nicholas finally found it. Itchy had given it to the baby, Oscar. And he couldn't even read yet! That didn't matter, though, because Itchy had chewed the book so badly that no one could read it anymore, anyway!

With so many people in the house, things were always in a mess. People were always borrowing Nicholas's crayons, and his pencils, and his toys . . . even his socks. He didn't even know how many he had anymore.

He thought and thought. What could he do to help his family with the mess? And then he had an idea. He would organize the house. He would count everything and make signs. He would make a sign for how many crayons he had, how many toy cars, and how many socks. Maybe he would even make a sign for Uncle Lloyd's T-shirts. When people wanted to borrow something, he could keep track of what was missing and who had it.

Nicholas started with his basket of crayons. He counted them all and then he made a sign: 37 crayons. He hung it on the basket. Then he counted his pencils. Ten pencils. He put a rubber band around them and made a sign for the can they were in. Then he counted the socks in his drawer. Nine pairs of socks. How many socks was that? He counted and then he made a sign for his sock drawer.

Henrietta saw what Nicholas was doing. "What a good idea," she said. "I'm going to do my room, too."

Then Violet did her room and soon everyone was busy. Petula and Delia organized their rooms, too. Uncle Lloyd and Grandma Eudora

organized the tools in the shed and all the food in the kitchen.

They even counted the jars of Oscar's baby food: six jars of bananas, ten jars of vegetables, and four jars of meat.

Itchy even organized his bones.

Soon there were signs everywhere.

"Can I borrow a pencil?" asked Delia.

"Sure thing," replied Nicholas with a smile as he crossed off the 10 and wrote 9. Then he wrote down Delia's name. "And now I know where it is," he said happily. And the next time he had a library book at home, he would know where that was, too!

Nicholas had solved the problem and helped his whole family. And that day Nicholas got a new name. They called him the Organizer.

Nicholas made a sign about that, too, and he taped it on his door. It said, "Nicholas Masloppy, the Organizer. Call me, and be the wiser!"

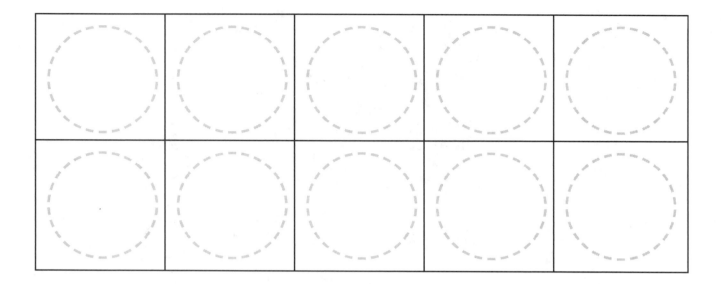

■ Make 15 copies of the above ten-frame using either overhead transparencies or paper and cut around them. Color with a black marker a set as shown below.

Names _____ Date _____

Total Number	Packs of 10	Loose	Packs of 5	Loose

- These game materials can be made more durable by pasting them on oaktag and laminating them.

- **Cut apart these loose stamps game pieces**

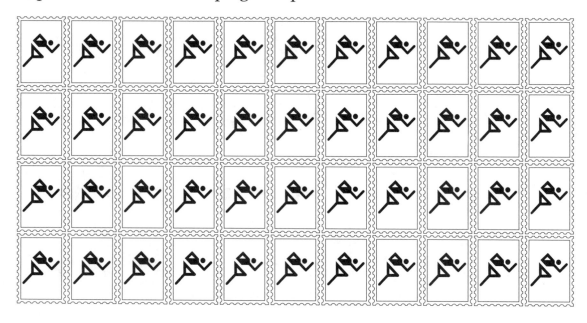

- **Cut out these Full Page game pieces**

■ Place your stamps on these ten pages of a stamp book. On each turn, figure:

How many stamps do you have now? How many stamp pages are full?

■ These cards can be made more durable by pasting them on oaktag and laminating them.

Set #1

4	9	10	13
16	18	20	22
26	27	31	33
39	40	43	46
48	51	56	57
62	65	69	70
73	78	82	85
87	90	98	100

■ These cards can be made more durable by pasting them on oaktag and laminating them.

Set #2

102	109	110	114
115	120	128	131
137	146	149	151
155	162	166	173
178	180	182	186
195	198	201	213
219	221	228	232
236	241	247	250

Names _____ Date _____

Number of stamps	+	Number of new stamps	=	new total